SMOULDER

SMOULDER

Poems by Mark Cox

David R. Godine · Publisher
Boston

First published in 1989 by
DAVID R. GODINE, PUBLISHER, INC.
Horticultural Hall
300 Massachusetts Avenue
Boston, Massachusetts 02115

Copyright © 1989 by Mark Cox

Library of Congress Cataloging in Publication Data

Cox, Mark, 1956–
Smoulder : poems / by Mark Cox.—1st ed.
p.   cm.
ISBN 0-87923-811-9.—ISBN 0-87923-814-3 (pbk.)
I. Title.
PS3553.093S66   1989   89-45390
811'.54—dc20   CIP

My thanks to the following periodicals wherein some of these poems first appeared:

The American Poetry Review: "The Lido," "Linda's House of Beauty," "Nothing Like us Ever Was," "Poem for the Name Mary"; *The Brooklyn Review:* "Long-lighted Evenings in the Garden"; *Calliope:* "Tell Us Everything You Know"; *Crazyhorse:* "Sorrow Bread"; *The Green Mountains Review:* "Geese"; *Goddard Review:* "The Will"; *The Grolier Poetry Prize Annual 1987:* "The Barbells of the Gods"; *The Indiana Review:* "It" (under the title "Crossings"), "Horizontals," "Prospect, Ohio," "Running My Fingers through My Beard on Bolton Road," "Why Is That Pencil Always Behind Your Ear"; *The North American Review:* "Fugitive Love"; *Poetry:* "I Want to Know What Love Is," "Simile at the Side of the Road," "Things My Grandfather Must Have Said": *Poetry Northwest:* "Divorce," "Putting on My Coat"; and *Willow Springs:* "Donald."

Some of these poems also appeared in a chapbook, *Barbells of the Gods,* published by Ampersand Press, 1988.

"The Barbells of the Gods," "Divorce," and "Geese" were reprinted in *The Midwest Review.*

I also wish to express my gratitude to the Mrs. Giles M. Whiting Foundation and the Vermont Council on the Arts for financial support received during the completion of this book.

And, finally, my thanks to the following people whose friendship and criticism helped make these poems possible: Nano Chatfield, Mark Doty, Keith Earnshaw, Carol Hamilton, Mary Greene, Mary La Chapelle, Ben Mitchell, Jack Myers, Leslie Ullman, Roger Weingarten, and David Wojahn.

For Rita

Contents

There is another world, but it is in this one.

—PAUL ELUARD

I can't see! I can't see! . . . I had my eyes closed . . .

—LARRY FINE

SMOULDER

The Word

I get in between the covers as quietly as I can.
Her hand is on my pillow and I put my face as close
as I can without waking her up. We made salad yesterday
and her fingertips still smell of green pepper and onions.
I feel homey, almost safe, breathing this, remembering
the way we washed the vegetables under cold water, peeled,
then sliced them with the harmless little knife her sister
gave us for Christmas. I feel childish and gently pull
the blanket over my head, barely touching my lips
to the short, ragged fingernails she chews while talking
to her mother on the phone. These days there's so much bad news
from home. Old people who keep living and living awfully,
babies who stop breathing for no reason at all.
I am so close to her that if I were to speak one word
silently, she would feel it and toss the covers to one side,
and for this reason I'll say nothing as long as I can.
Let the sheet stiffen above us, I have nothing to say.
Not about their lives or my own life.
Not about the branches so weighted with snow
they don't brush our window anymore.
Not about the fact that the only way I can touch anymore
at all, the only way I can speak, is by trying not to.
"What's left, what's left, what's left," my dog breathes
in his sleep. Lately I snore badly in a language
only he understands. I've been trying so hard to teach,
I've been trying so hard to switch bodies
with the young people in my classes that last week, when the dog
woke me and wanted to go out, I took his face in my hands
and told him not to be afraid. "You know so much already," I said.
"You are talented and young, you have something to give people,
I wouldn't lie to you."
Rita told this story as we sat around the salad with friends,
repeating again and again how the dog closed his eyes and basked.
Sleep is also the only place I can type with more than three
fingers, I said. But I thought, it's true, all this,

3

I speak best and most fully in my sleep. When my heart
is not wrapped in layer after layer of daylight, not prepared
like some fighter's taped fist.
She sleeps, her hand next to my mouth, the number
for the 24-hour bank machine fading on its palm.
The word starts briefly from between my lips, then turns back.
The word sifts deeper into what my life is.

The Barbells of the Gods

It's a Thursday, getting late,
and we're the last three cars in the lot.
Richard has his face in his golf clubs
like they're flowers and smell nice,
and Buster is already talking bowling balls and shoes,
talking us slowly out of summer,
when Rich looks up sideways and says he's never been
with one man long enough to watch a pair of jeans fade
and what's it like being married to women?
Out on the lake there's that kind of silence that's loud—
two suns moving towards each other, one perfect, the other
just a glare—and I clean and jerk one last beer
and we talk about desire,
but nobody here, our legs dangling over fenders,
knows what he wants or how to get it any more
than when we were kids
and girls spent their adolescence as the hood ornament
of some boy's father's car. It's too
complicated, Buster says.
And he means the rule book is immense,
that there doesn't seem to be a clear point
or object to him.
But I say, You must have dreams of growing old
with one person
and how has it been so hard, pardon the pun,
no offense, to find the right guy? . . .
I did, Richard breaks in, but he's married,
so that's kind of why I'm asking you.
And I say, oh,
and Buster says, let's go someplace noisy
where we can really talk

Things My Grandfather Must Have Said

I want to die in the wintertime,
make the ground regret it,
make the backhoe sweat.

January. Blue Monday
after the holiday weekend.
I want it to be hard on everybody.

I want everyone to have a headache
and the traffic to be impossible.
Back it up for miles, Jesus.

I want steam under the hood, bad directions,
cousins lost, babies crying, and sleet.
I want a wind so heavy their umbrellas howl.

And give me some birds, pigeons even,
anything circling for at least half an hour,
and plastic tulips and a preacher who stutters

"Uh" before every word of Psalm 22.
I want to remind them just how bad things are.
Spell my name wrong on the stone, import

earthworms fat as Aunt Katie's arms
and put them under the folding chairs.
And I want a glass coffin,

I want to be wearing the State of Missouri
string tie that no one else liked. . . . God,
I hope the straps break

and I fall in with a thud. I hope
the shovel slips out of my son's hands.
I want them to remember I don't feel anything.

I want the food served straight from my garden.
I want the head of the table set. I want
everyone to get a pennant that says,

"Gramps was the greatest,"
and a complete record of my mortgage payments
in every thank-you note.

And I want to keep receiving mail for thirteen years,
all the bills addressed to me,
old friends calling every other month

to wonder how I am.
Then I want an earthquake or rising water-table,
the painful exhumation of my remains.

I want to do it all again.

I want to die the day before something truly
important happens and have my grandson say:
What would he have thought of that.

I want you all to know how much I loved you.

Where

This last time I am touching you tentatively,
then withdrawing awed, as the first worms
to find our bodies will. I am looking
for happiness and sadness,
the invisible kingdoms where they reside.
A people in New Guinea claim that intellect
lies in the larynx and only in voice
is the truth known. We speak
of the heart, the navel, the portholes of our eyes;
but today I am thinking with my fingers,
remembering the first woman to guide them,
and the fact that she has three children now
while I have none, and that after so many years without
an "accident," I have to doubt I ever will.
Your breasts are like drifting clouds, I see
something new in them every time you breathe.
But they are not where the happiness is.
Your abdomen is a series of hills. Yet that, also,
is not where happiness is.
Your hand is a white horse, perfectly satisfied
to pull quietly at the darkening grass.
The blue vein in your thigh is where it drinks.
And the artery pulsing nearby
is the rest of the herd terrified
into the canyon of my hand
where the sadness will be tomorrow.

Sorrow Bread

The trees were backlit, like a Sunday school play,
and as the sun went down behind the quarry,
a spider made his way around and around
one leaf on a sapling next to them, playing out
the thread by which a spider keeps itself in the world,
drawing together that slick, green leaf
into an inverted cone meant to shed the coming rain.
The man thought of the carefully folded wax paper
they'd eaten their sandwiches from. He thought of each
crumpled piece relaxing back into a square
in the dark of the knapsack beside them.

Below, rings appeared on the water in the quarry,
and even after she felt the rain she claimed
it was a host of fingerling bluegill and bass, free now
to come up and mouth the cooling surface. "No,
that's rice," he said, "rice from heaven. Happy anniversary."

This took place in Indiana, which is a state I know well.
I know the woods and the quarries, and how it feels
to be walking in the woods and have the forest give way.
It delighted me, staring down into quarries.

The man and woman sat at the edge for a very long time,
so that when they rose to go home, her legs had gone to sleep.
He put his arm around her, supporting her. She grinned
and said, "You must feel like this when you sit on the toilet
reading for so long." He was a minister. She was a nurse.
For awhile, they looked at the smiles on each other's faces.
Then she thought it was all right, that they'd just have to go slowly.
And he let go of her, reached down for their knapsack.

I painted bridges for a living once, and once
I felt my rigging tremble, and looked up to see
my partner falling away from me. I know that work
and what it feels like to walk into work with somebody
day after day. My partner loved to drink beer for lunch, sit
right next to the juke box and sing. He wanted to be a rock star

but he hit the ground on his side, like a little boy
who'd just been tucked into bed. And at the height
I watched from, the sound his body made seemed
a childish moan of regret, as if it were summer,
and too early to be dark.

What do you do when there's nothing you can do, but
you can't just do nothing? When you've coexisted easily
with time, and then, suddenly, there's no time,
followed by the flood of too much? It took so long
to get to him, each thud of my boots echoing
in the bottomlessness of my head.

Another time, I was holding a rope that snapped; no one
got hurt, but I remember holding onto that useless end
long after it looked silly to be doing so. On deep nights,
at least some of them, I dream I'm still there: flat
on my ass with my feet braced against the guardrail,
trying to live up to obligations that aren't valid anymore.
What am I doing but saving myself? Maybe
that rope tied to nothing was actually holding me up
during the long fall my soul took
as friends' heads swung from sight.
Maybe the all or nothing of it all
was working its way into my hands like a cramp,
making certain I'd never forget how easy dying is.

The nurse opened her eyes once and saw him weeping,
searching her wrist for a pulse. Perhaps she thought,
Now I know what I looked like to the people I cared for.

I knew none of these people, really. I never asked
if my young partner wanted kids, or what he would do
with a million dollars. The reverend and his wife led
the church of some old friends in Indianapolis, who told me
about the accident over the phone. But I was moved somehow,
and as I sat on the porch watching our spiders arrange
their nets in the shrubs, I began to see both incidents clearly.
And I saw the husband, hoarse from begging a forest for help,
have to choose between staying and going.

Rita came home home then—after being in Connecticut for a day
and a half — wanting to play, say hello, and hold each other —
but I stayed where I was, circling the piece of paper
and these random events, until she turned off the lights
of the screened porch, trying to get a reaction.
I said "please" twice, then screamed, "I'm writing out here!"
so loudly that it echoed three times in the valley around us.
I moaned, *Why is she doing this? A thread like this only happens
once or twice a year.* How puny my voice must have seemed
to any neighbor; what a statement to have drift in
while you're washing dishes or reading the newspaper.

My partner survived and within two years was painting bridges again.
He lives in Missouri, which is, like Indiana, someplace
I used to think I knew well. The nurses at the hospital liked him,
because he was considerate, and never complained
or was angry with them for doing their jobs.

I should stop this now, before the first few drops of rain
begin darkening the sill, and climb the slick stairs toward bed
where I know the woman I love is waiting for an explanation.
"It's me," I should say to the dog in the doorway, "I'll take it
from here." Then again, I would say anything to make myself
feel less helpless, to extract good from bad; I would say anything
to go on, and need to admit that outright.

I've tried hard, looking down at this rope, to love the knots
I slide down to, to see other hands than mine there;
but it is my rope and no one else's.
Everyone has their own rope, and each reaches the end
in his own sweet time.

Prospect, Ohio

Awakening to a strange room, I may open
my eyes and see him: the twilight
of the burner tracing haze across our kitchen,
the coffee coming to in its pot.
In the near darkness he coughs once, quietly,
as if from far below me.

To these places I carry the old smell of quilts.
I am ten and my nose is cold
and in a dim room my uncle sits dressed for the train,
coughing so quietly in the clean, blue light
that it sounds like he's already left.

What does this mean? How long
will I dream of myself fluttering in that doorway?
Back upstairs, wound in thick bedding,
I begin to suspect the truth:
he is waiting. His brother's kitchen is warm,
the cigar smoke and steam swirl beautifully
in the light of stars, and he waits
as if to claim himself should he appear.

Years later, in Columbus and a motel tub,
the water so still my ash drifts complete
to its bottom, I'm still drawn to this.
A little water drips from my elbow,
a circle of orange pulses on the faucet, and I know
he neither slept nor wakened — that
the startled return of daylight,
the shuffling room to room,
the amniotic nights, were whole in themselves.
That I haven't been waiting at all.

Nothing Like Us Ever Was

Much fabled by tissue poachers, sought after by chicken wire
traders and fading coaches, this is where floats go to die.

Instinctively they know, as the maroon bleeds into the white,
and coast here to fall on their sides, feet in the air.

What — Innocence? Energy? Or merely hollow ideas to be heartily
applauded once? Huge things built in warehouses owned by parents

where somehow it was always fall and cold. Warmed by bottled gas
torpedoes, built in fits and starts by fingertips hurt and raw

from the wire mesh skeletons and twist-ties of our existence
and each other. For my part, I couldn't get my ladder close enough

to hers. And above us, like Hawaiian gods, football helmets with faces
in them, half-formed papier-mâché, some painted tennis balls for eyes—

what a project becoming us was. And yes, the clapping does ring
hollow now, having to admit I thought corsages grew in iceboxes

and long ago used our class motto to wipe the dipstick. Little
wire cables on pulleys making our hands move up and down. Hello.

Good-bye. And while the sun bounced from one carefully washed car to
another, from trombone to trumpet to tuba and back, on the other side

of that world recent graduates were suiting up for a final quarter
our coaches still can't admit we lost. Ladies and gentlemen,

renting that fountain for the punch was a nice touch, don't you think?
We keep happening over and over.

Listening to My Stomach

The knees of our houses buckle. Windows
go dull with curtains, then fail completely.
Ominous, threading smoke from the brick stacks of town.
Are we retaliating,

or has winter just brought its murderous lips close —
kicking the snow up into a silver-plated twirl
around that crescent moon thumbed back in a crowd of tin stars
like something I can't quite put my finger on?

At one point in my life,
the sun was a bright orange dot about 22 inches
down the barrel from my right eye,
and in the time it took to set behind the hills
I could field dress the whole goddamn world.
By noon, the river gurgled like a slit throat.
Dusk was a blue just beneath the skin of everything.

Tonight, again, it seems I've scooped out
the daylight with my bare hands,
ending up in an all-night diner over a steaming heap of breakfast
while a fleet of snowplows scrape the interstate,
and a herd of trucks sleeps fitfully in the parking lot.

Here, at the edge of the losing continent of my neighborhood,
there are dogs lapping at puddles in the slush,
slinking from one dim backyard to the next
with a concentration we reserve for chess and adultery,
while I remain insomniac, holstered
in a vinyl booth just trying to decide
if we are brief noises living in an ocean of silence
or complete silences living on an island of noise.

On a night like this, once, the first girl I paid for
took one of my ears completely into her mouth.
I don't know what I expected — maybe
the long echo of fucking,
or me hearing myself hearing —

maybe I thought I would really hear her then —
but what I recognized was the rumble of a gunboat
powering through her head, some 18-year-old
steering with his crotch, and adjusting the binoculars
while five different plans crisscrossed behind him,

and then the sound of that protracted adolescent wake
slapping up against the seawall of his town —
cold and sudden as moonlight after clouds,
as an uncle's palm when he puts down his beer
just to hit you.

You know how it is, half-lying around after a big meal,
listening to your stomach —
though you can liken it to the ruminance of harmless animals,
you know you kill and hunker down.

Geese

We were in love and his uncle had a farm
where he took me hunting
to try to be in love even more.

He wanted me to have what he had:
black coffee,
toast buttered with bad light
in a truck stop splotched with smoke,

then moonlight on the hills and snow
like a woman stepping out of her dress.

And it was good even as we killed it.
The stalks lightening,
the sun rising like a worn, yellow slicker
over us, bent over panting
because it wasn't hit cleanly
and had run us both dizzy
before settling down.

There was a particular knife he used
to make the asshole bigger.
After that, one could just reach in
and remove anything that wasn't necessary,

and thinking about it now, I see
the old school desk behind his uncle's house
put there for that reason,
see my husband sadly hosing it down,
as if regretting how and what men are taught . . .

I'm lying . . .
Though the diner I see belongs
in a small town where I went to school,
the desk had no drawers, was in fact a table,
and he was whistling as he washed it.

The sun didn't rise
like something to keep the rain off us;
it hung, like a cold chandelier
in which I could see each filament
in each flame-shaped bulb
beating itself senseless against the light —
brilliant and hollow,

beautiful and inhumane . . .
But I wanted so badly
to forgive his hands, forgive his lovers,
and to forget how, driving home, I was fooled
by half an acre of decoys
and some camouflage netting,

how I wanted to honk but didn't,
and how the whole scene made me realize
that mannequins mate for life too,
in department stores, wearing back-to-school clothes,

made me remember that if you press hard enough
on a bird's dead breast, it will betray its own kind,
that when he took its neck and broke it
I said his first name.

The Pale and Hairless Ankles of the Sun

On Wednesdays I can't breathe right.
As if my tongue were a clenching fist.
Whatever I'd like you to hear me say then
is too much larger than I am.
Wednesdays — I can't bear them.
They're like coffins surfacing
from deep in my blood.
They're like logs so immense
you can't get your arms around them;
I can't carry them inside.
And Thursdays! Today, not one kind word
and the newspaper was so heavy
it disappeared into the ground.
It caused my legs to fall asleep.
Wednesdays want so much to be saved
that each one pulls more sky in after it.
Each Thursday has more earth in its mouth.

I Want To Know What Love Is

The dent in the bed is shaped like a valley of a river
and I am back on my haunches above it, trying to get
a morning started, poking at the fog with a stick.

Last night we opened the tin can with no label here
on a sharp rock and ate it with our fingers, saying:
Sometimes it's just cold and you can't see anything.

A light rain threads down through the trees — the blue
caress of static in the wet light of a stereo.

Someday we'll be old and grey and full of sleep
and no longer worried about the pantry.
My dreams will be of cutting my own hair, of leaving
my own body blinded and bound between pillars.

We won't unroll these runners out of social clubs,
barbeques, and low-lit bars. I will walk only to the 7-11
to buy cigarettes and ask the salesgirls if I'm handsome.

A thin rope of smoke plays out upward and with
my free hand I hold my collar closed at the neck.

This stick in my hand is the question
I wanted to ask you.

The Lido

The Lido Hotel was painted blue, to look cool,
I guess, an almost pool-water blue,
which in Freetown, Sierra Leone, could only be a plus.
The ride in was so horrid, the buses and lorries
so cramped and close
that I could lean against the air conditioner in our room
till my navel almost froze to it,
watching the heat waves through the one window's blinds,
and thinking it hadn't been so bad to be twenty-two and lying
around in a West African hotel with avocadoes and a book.
It was *The Tin Drum*, and in the time it took to finish it
Simone could have walked the whole city, the slap
of her rubber thongs tapping from market to market, to the doctor
and back, twice in two days. I never saw anything. I never knew
anything. I was deeply connected to that room, so lost
in Grass's novel and the one I wanted to write that nothing
short of the hazy, blue and pink cocktail sunset
could even get the shades up.
I sat there still as bottled water on a dresser,
whose plastic was also blue and inviting:
I soaked in that solitude like a stone.

The baby came in August, which is a rainy month,
and I couldn't use the motorcycle so we had no doctor.
The tenth day was the worst
and not even sweet Momoh who swept our porch
would come near because of the screams.
It was born with a fever. The midwives
dipped it in water that had run from the roof.
The rain came down like nails on the roof, and I turned

twenty-three while Simone covered her ears with her hands
and sang to the screaming little boy who may or may not
have wanted to live. He did for two weeks, and after the first
stopped crying, just lay there in himself. Will you believe me
if I say his eyes were blue, Tropicana Las Vegas pool-water blue?

And the question becomes: what month were we in Freetown,
yes? Are we the parents or the children
of our grief, was I recovering from or walking toward
the unreal heat, and have I ever managed to put that book down?
And what about all the hotel rooms since
and what about Simone out walking slapping walking? . . .
It's hell to be young and full of wishfulness.
It's a bitch to be old and sweeping someone else's porch, too.
But neither quite compares to seeing that baby's eyes,
which were brown
when I opened them.

Fugitive Love

Fused this way, naked and back to back, wrenched
in and out of love, he could be trying to say something,
she could be trying not to listen. It seems

important to know and I don't;
I doubt even Rodin did and anyway,
times like that, to say anything

is to say too much.
I think Rodin saw them as twins,
Siamese and fraternal, connected

and yet not. Longing
for more and less of the same.

At the cafeteria today, I saw two lovers
forget to pick up trays. They were so involved
with everything they didn't expect anything.

➤

Opposite me, on the other side of the sculpture,
another man and another woman. I can't tell
if they're together really. How long, or if,

they've known each other at all.
The look in his eyes is the look of a man
who has come a far way to say something simple —
mouth half-open, eyes half-closed —

and I'm trying to imagine them like this forever,
just their clothes touching,
and how it will feel for them in the back of the taxi
that even now may be moving across the city.

Maybe the seams of their pants legs will touch
or the sides of the soles of their shoes.
And one will think, *please touch me so I can leave.*
And one will think, *please don't touch me so I can leave.*

Outside — a harsh light all over everything,
buildings rippling in their lustrous skin,

➤

and someone else might call it Fear
and someone else might name it "the tearing and merging of clouds,"

but this has everything to do with her.
There are times when that's the way it goes with souls.
Back to back. Fruitless.

There are moments when the soul
seems more physical than the body, no one hears anyone
and saying anything is just a bronze scream.

And maybe this is what the man
in the sculpture is feeling and why he looks
as if he's boiling alive in the air around them
and why I don't think he's trying to speak at all.

It

Some feelings are like daylight seen from the ocean floor,
dim like that and beyond me.
A porch light wound in fog, the fog wound in darkness.
A voice from the fog saying, *Tell me what you feel*
when you die like that for each other, when you arch
your backs to bridge the story between us and

I can't — no, I can explain, it's like
my father with a slashed throat, at first, when I feel
like this, and I'm on my knees over his whitening face,
and I try to hold the slippery ends of that artery
together, I try to right things. It's like leaning out
over all that is familiar to you
and finding it isn't
and there's nothing that can be done for it,
with all the tools love has given you,
still there's nothing except this gradual draining, until
even my own hands grow cool and hollow. And if I touch

your face like this, if I touch your cheek just below the eye
it's because I'm trying so hard to remember what resilience is.
God, I don't want to die before I figure this out.
With no one to bend over my empty face
saying, "I knew him, he could breathe, damn it,
he could move his hand and touch a face with the best of them." So,

I can't really explain it, I guess. I can't explain why the sound
of my own heart is not enough, why these nights in the fog I need
another pulse and another dim skin. I can't explain this urge
to pour my life out rhythmically onto the ground
and see my own face reflected in my own story.
Or how the world looks staring over me with its anxious trees and
its stars pacing. Or how the wind coughs into me and the leaves
ripple across my blood toward you. Woman,

why can't I let the magician make his two ropes one?
Though there is no sweeter stone to hold in my mouth,
no larger shell to work into, still, there is no
higher homage I can pay you than this callused thumb,
wet with the dark ink and doubt of my family.

Sleep. Outside,
the fog is like hair. The fog is a luminous forearm
or a chiffon dress gone damp with dancing
and thrown over the back of a chair. You were asleep
when it finally put its hands to the window.

In This His Suit

Not his clothes, but their chimerical creases.
Not his body, but the gestures of his body
worn last and put unpressed
into its plastic. Not the hand,
but how he held it, palm buttressing head.
Not the meat, not words, but grace; not the mouth,
but the smoke, scratches on a plate, the
table's dulled edge.
Not absence, not presence. Not indentation,
but impression. Not not, but not is; not either
or neither. The hose's curve, the garden's
mounds, the slab walk's slope, the smell of the smell,
the sound of the sound, the book's missing page
found in another book.
Not the death, but his dying.
Not male, not female, not young, old, compassionate,
bitter, peaceful, or sorrowed.
Not the life, but the living.

Horizontals

"Forgive me, no don't forgive me, no forgive me,"
Big Bird was saying. He'd promised

to guard the orange juice with his life, then fallen asleep.
It was a marathon, fuzzy beings wearing numbers and gasping things

like "Thanks, I needed that" or "I feel like a new creature,"
once they stuck their noses into his friend's o.j.

I was kind of dozing in my chair, in fact, sprawled,
like I'd been pasted there by an explosion,

with I. A. Richards open on my lap, a weak, rainy
sunlight from the west in my face,

but it seemed selfish watching *Sesame Street*
and thinking about poetries and sciences

while hearing my dog's feet scrape the floor as he slept,
so I got down on all fours and put my head on him,

and made believe his heart was a shutter,
loose and banging against the house,

and that the blood slogging ceaselessly
through the roads of his body was weather.

I think I came to understand there's only one storm,
it just keeps circling the earth till it gets to us again,

and that the pounding I felt even in my hair the first time
you innocently brushed it back

was just two ordinary clouds boiling over that edge
where what we can't see stops and starts

and slamming into each other
with an inevitability we'd eventually have to imitate.

Just the valves of our hearts opening and closing,
a brief flash in the eye lighting up our yards,

then drizzle, guilt, sorrow,
those adjusters we've come to know by first names,

looking at our houses, our spouses,
with their tiny notepads, with pencils behind their ears,

but in the end with no real end to point to,
no line chalked on the road where they can say some

time was beaten or a tape was broken. Just more
weather, pale and uncertain, stopping to retie its shoes —

Forgive me. I slept so well. Forgive me.

The Good and The Icky

"First we drive to the bread store,"
my daughter insists, walking
with exaggerated casualness to the cupboard.
Apparently her friend is sniffing the air
because she stops suddenly, saying *"Yes,
don't you just love the way it smells."*
She will be all grown-up before she gets
this sandwich made, but that's OK, it's
the methodical anticipation she lives for,
not the crusty knife or jelly lid so sticky
she'll need help to open it.
While my ex-husband mauls a girl in her twenties,
while the dog angles its nose up to the counter,
she is savoring the chosen ingredients
in all their culinary separateness, the options
lined up in her head like people waiting at the check-out.
When I was young could I see the whole list at once?
The good and the icky, label to label, and lapel to lapel?
Did it give me pleasure to be given the long scroll
of grocery store receipt and to clutch it as I rode backward
out the automatic door toward a station wagon
that could hold anything?
Could I have once squealed in stores, appreciating
even the tiny print of weight and measure,
or thrilled, because, as my daughter says,
"it's like being inside the chandelier —
you can have any color you want"?
Lately, the men from United Parcel stand too close
when I sign for what they've brought to me,
the three boys scaping my land have the very same back,
and the sound of utensils clicking into place
can seat me at the kitchen table for hours.
These days, while my daughter offers imaginary water
to her imagined friend, I recall my own mother
and the rattle of ice in her glass.

The Angelfish

Every day at five, the beautiful angelfish stops
at this corner of the tank. He is patient
and knows the bartender will come
with his salt shaker of food.

Every so often he glances around to see
if a certain female angelfish has come in.

He thinks about how if I stare at a woman long enough,
she will either blush or not and I will either blush
or not. It strikes him that fish don't have much weather
to talk about and he wonders if I know my mouth
is opening and closing all the time.

Does he love her? Does she prefer another angelfish
in another section of the huge tank? Will he ever
be happier than this? The bartender sees him now
and smiles and puts his big face up to the glass.

Something dry, the angelfish says, *something very dry.*

31

Keepers

My son, the director, tells Mommy to stand here
and hold this doily like a net —
the biggest fish in all the seas of all the world
will be happening through the living room momentarily.
I'm to get my knife ready and start the grill.

In one hand he's dragging a baseball bat
with some string wrapped around it, in the other
he just barely holds the bathroom scale. "We'll need this
to weigh its velocity," he says, and when I suggest
that the biggest fish in the world just might have teeth,
he smiles and pulls an oven mitt
from beneath his Hulk Hogan pajamas.

God, which direction would you like me to face when I scream out
how much I love this child? Is there a particular posture
to be assumed, a certain pitch attained, or vibrato matched?
The neighbor girl we sit for is a giggle down the hall,
disembodied, with her hand on a doorknob
wanting to know if his parents are ready yet.

Late last night, across the valley, a neighbor's cat finally met
something that could stalk as well as it,
and the screams were horrible, spilled out onto the breeze
from the body itself. A single barn swallow woke to do battle,
then spent half an hour celebrating,
and as I thought of the vacillating whistle it made in the dark,
I forced myself to think of screams as music: orchestrated, scripted,
offered up to paying public as the only opera that counts.
Was I wrong to hope it was the tabby and not the black one
Isaac loves? Was it wrong to favor a pregnant merciless being
over an old merciless being?

The brick barbeque pit looks like a throne in the moonlight.
Momentarily, the dog will trip into the room
wearing my green bathrobe and looking terrifically confused,
trying for all he's worth to get at the milk bone
on the string's end. "There," Zack will say,
and something will come over me and I'll start sharpening
the plastic picnic knife on the sliding door, humming
with purposeful menace until my son throws his arms
around the spaniel screaming, "It's just Mr. Shivers, Dad."

God, I know we'll sing a great duet — what'll it take
to make you throw us both back?

Burritos

Four A.M., roughly half of humanity sleeping,
and my estimate, not including box springs,
is that if you stacked all the mattresses in the world
you'd have to climb up their flimsy plastic handles
150,000 miles to go to bed.
Think of that — hand over hand and when you got there
the moon would be right in your face.

As the light strengthens I can feel my own weight more,
the chair I'm propped on starts to take shape beneath me.
There are my hands, they've been on my knees,
and now here come the bones that were in both yesterday.
Do we get more separate than this?
In what little sleep I got I dreamed

that I was pregnant, tucked between the sheets, garnished
with melted cheese — interpret that one, Herr Gelusil.
The old dog is making puppy noises in *his* sleep;
I haven't got a clue about who he's talking to in there.
Betty just cursed my name in broken Spanish . . .

When she was pregnant with Jamie (who's sleeping
down the hall and has screamed "I'm not afraid"
twice since about two o'clock), I'd lie awake like this —
with my head on them and the dog's head on me —
and it seemed like even with heartburn
we were a regular family . . .

The dog must know his dying will be steady and slow.
Jamie must have realized I can't protect him anymore.
Once again, I've put off telling Betty
what she already knows.

Divorce

Like deeply chained buoys, languid and backlit by a neon sign,
they're still dancing to slow ones in the rear of the bar.

Old friends, as you said, come here to "do drinks," throw darts,
and "connect" with each other,

couples who have the feel of having known each other
for "longish" times,

before this place got popular with younger crowds.
Not old, of course, most aren't much older than you and I,

but still, with that weathered, companionable look
that marriage gives you

and five daiquiris can't take away —
like that tie you loosened, but could not bring yourself to undo

so you just slipped it over your head twice a day. And if now,
having made it, you're thinking, *Well, yet another glass raised*

against end-rhyme and Love's tailored, dry-cleaned noose;
another zipper lowered on upwardly mobile values,

all the better when I try to explain that I've never seen you
look so lonely in your whole half-life as a moment ago,

slipping past that bald guy — whose cigarette, incidentally,
you put out with your coat — playing darts back there,

dancing simultaneously and cheek-to-cheek with a wife
who'll need surgery to get out of her clothes.

One slow turn and he'll aim, throw the third and last,

then gently pat her ass

until she unlocks her arms, lets him go out a channel
between the pretzels and ivory-colored drink

she holds in respective hands.
For your birthday, all you wanted was to get to the bathroom,

and were making headway, until our waitress drove you against them.
And him, he swayed a little, then caught again

on the rhythm, reached down between their chests for matches
and craning his head behind hers relit the stub in his mouth,

while, as if you'd caused some immeasurable disturbance, seeming
to hold her even tighter for a moment,

dancing her away toward the round and tortured board,
not wanting to know if there was a hole in your life or not,

a black smudge to remember as meaning
one shouldn't, but has to, get close to love as that.

Putting on My Coat

Brother-in-law, the door of your death
is hung in such a way that it closes
but won't quite catch
and the act of approaching it
will open it.

Hinges whine. Fine cobwebs billow
against the hairs of our arms.
Peering around that casement into nothing,
our eyes unfold as slowly, as roselike, as two
crumpled fists of paper in the shadow of a desk.

And though mere grief takes in the smell of silence,
and though everywhere we put our hands
we touch each other's hands,
it's simply hard to pass through.

Not that you need me to tell you. On this side,
five inches of wet snow and a sun pale enough
to make the dog howl. Across the narrow street,
about halfway down her walk, your wife

leans against a brand new scoop, props her forehead
on her mittens on its handle, breathes
in short bursts, wipes her nose.

Last night, it took her lover three tries to get his car door shut
and the snowball he threw at the streetlight arced across my window.
It's falling leisurely. She's looking back at the house.

She'll survive. It's just that the farther two objects are from her,
the harder it is to distinguish the distance between them.

Her first love and her last.
Your death and her own. So close together now it seems,

as smoke twists above the chimney, the sun
fumbles in its glove box for the garage door opener.

What she can't forget is combing out your hair.
That like snow, each day the sheets around you seemed smoother.
That like shoveling, every day
she hears the faint rasp you came to.
That like the knob of a door to a room you didn't want to leave
was how you touched her face.

Poem for the Name Mary

Like smoke in a bottle, like
hunger, sometimes light fits,
wraps itself around a person
or thing and doesn't let go.
The light becomes a name,
and that name becomes a voice
through which light speaks to us.
Maybe this is what a friend means
when she says there is a pair of lips
in the air, maybe this is desire
and need too. Or maybe
this is just how to love a potato,
how to see what the potato sees:
the childish, white arms that reach out
through its eyes into the dark of our cabinets
to bless them.

Linda's House of Beauty

is on the left, twelve minutes south of the black and white
cows, and two passing zones shy of where the bicycle man
will rest before the hill. In one hand he will hold his
milk gallon of water. In the other, the orange hunter's
cap I just saw on the ground. Here, I know where I am —
the place I am one song short of. Tuesday,

I was looking at the ground, and when I pulled against
the door a woman was pushing it from the other side.
That surprised me and there was an odd feeling in my face
all the way to the cows. As if I wanted to smile
and drink at the same time, the way that cows seem
to want to say something while they chew.
That day my fourteen-year-old saliva, the water that broke

the moment.I was ready to be born, rearranged itself
in an astonishing sky. And I was guessing
she'd just come from Linda's.
She held a bottle of wine in both hands against
the new curve of her belly. There were thin lines
of snow along the stone fences
of the fields behind us.

I could be doing other things. I could drive a school bus
or make donuts. Or read gauges at the North Pole
for everybody. I could pedal slowly past the cows
and sing out to them like the old bicycle man.
Because I think that woman loved me for that moment.
I think the candles she must have lit that night
smelled like knee-high, unmown grass,

and when her husband messed her hair up she understood
I loved her back.

White Tornado

In commercials it spirals from room to room:
bread crumbs, bacon grease, fingerprints
get erased and you don't have to do anything.
Just unscrew the cap and get out of the way.
When it's over, even the lady's dress is clean,
her hair has been done, and sunlight streams
all at once into the kitchen like a happy child
with flowers.

Like hell, he thinks. Everybody knows
that memory is just a vacuum cleaner
with a filter we can't replace —
it spews out as much as it can take in, clarify,
so you work hard forever
in a haze you just get used to.

Most dust is human skin — sprinkles
on the vanilla cone of survivorship, sustenance
for the little fish who can't cut it on the bottom.
You do what you know — burning your fingers
on thin Styrofoam cups, parting your mouth
against the small bowl of a shaving mirror —
while they roll to one side
and float helplessly up through you
toward the silken scoop of forgiveness
on its wire handle.

After the *Today Show*, he will proceed to the medicine cabinet.
He'll wave like a mother at a summer camp bus,
its mirror will be free of the lint of her . . .
But it's hard having nothing to lean against but the sink.
And though there'll be nothing he can't see then,
he'll be all that is.

Archaic Torso of My Uncle Phil

Our broadcast day is over, I've unplugged
but there's still that perfect white dot
in the middle of the sky, still the smeary glow
of some distant transmission. What it reminds me of
is that bluish, phosphorescent dye they inject into you
before they stick the telescope up your astronomy. It's
the historyectomy of it, the rise and fall of the Roman
pulse rate, the existential yet plotted course
of our little dippers, that makes it so objectionable.
Some days I feel change coming on, but can't
tell if it's an airplane or my neighbor's chainsaw;
other days I just feel doomed. And tonight,
I'm certain I have both feet in the same sock,
that the moon is a head mirror on an Egyptian priest,
and a woman in Philadelphia
is carving the longboat with my name on it.
My whole body is a womb.
I'll miss everybody.
It hurts all over.

Milk Teeth

They're tender, these romantic film openings: light
confused, like a harmless animal, in some filmy curtains,
a sword blade of shadow between the sleeping bodies,
the two lovers retreating even at the moment they're
furthest apart — eyes closed, mouths parted, the flowers
on their pillow slips seeming to blossom from their hair.

His keys, her lighter, his watch, her earrings,
unlumping, becoming autonomous on the bed stand —
Was that a car not-starting or a bird singing?
And beyond, is that the solitary mower
circling his gas can in an ever-expanding ripple?
Was that a newspaper thumping or a massage manual
falling open off the end of the bed?

Chapter One: What to Do When You're Thirty-Two and Haven't
Figured Out How to Touch Another Human Being Correctly Yet?
The lovers nuzzle and gurgle, giving us the distinct impression
they're keeping eyes closed on purpose now.
Who are they holding? What original curvature
have they formed to?
And given up themselves for?

God, I remember fearing this — thirteen and still wetting the bed,
terrified I wouldn't stop in time to savor such moments,
would have to stay up all night sneaking off to the bathroom
or else sleep horribly,
like in those research films of couples snoozing,
where the camera watches them change position all night,
hilarious at high speeds:

He lands a roundhouse, cups his hand around her mouth, gets
an elbow that glances off one rib. The sheet goes slack between
his legs and when she flips, one knee finds the crotch, digs in and
persists until he murmurs "hmmm" and she murmurs "hmmm,"
while meantime ever so minimally beneath the snow-white sheets
her tampon is leaking and his pubes are detaching,
and their toenails are snagging and the perfume on their pillows
has them both coughing and gagging

though it looks like they've thumbed through *The Kama Sutra*,
willing to try anything: gender reversals, regressions, projections;
timid approaches, reproaches, rejections; nose scratching, crotch
cupping, lip licking, drooling . . . Small wonder one wakes
either refreshed or wringing wet and either way swings right out
on the nearest side.

➤

Saturday morning, sworn to silence, we'd dress,
make our beds, lace our half-height leather boots
in the bright sails our windows cast on the floor,
empty the books from our knapsacks and pack
for the voyage we'd planned secretly during prayers.

The grapes we hadn't eaten for lunch, the cookies
it had taken such effort to save, were the supplies
we now estimated our arrival by — all smiles at being
up early and not on the way to school, unaccountably happy
at the thought of our sleeping father, how he'd wake

to find our moorings long loosed. I remember that feeling
just as well as I now know the feelings those sleeping adults
carried with them from their dreams. There's always,
counting sheep, a wolf somewhere to be reckoned with.
"As an individual grows older, he grows more unique from, not

like his fellows," somebody said. I'm pretty sure he said this
just before getting out of bed, wondering who was lying
next to him and why, in that first moment before opening his eyes,
when we too often feel like empty boots, untied and slack-tongued,
buried to the eyelets in mud that won't let go, the part of us

that has to stay behind, unevolved, stubborn, needing to be taken
instead of simply held. Even if we were only children and even
if the sea were only a small backyard, and the porch where we raised
our anchor only separated inches from the house it led to,
didn't we go then, fully and without regret, without

bodies that ached as if for some archetypal pain to give meaning
to pain itself? Didn't we go, ecstatic, across and into
an unfamiliar name and drink straight from the soda bottle without
wiping it first? Wasn't there hope then of navigating the fence,
rounding and entering through a front door

that had been altered forever, to a father married forever
and a strange girlfriend made wife and mother?
There are still moments I sail —
and to be honest, it only happens in women —
there are still moments I wake and don't want my fuck back,

want, in fact, to cast off again,
and am not the Bakers' dog digging its own shallow grave
and lying in it, circling and circling
while the shadows move slowly as glaciers toward it,

➤

but rather, wake to find it's Saturday, springtime,
the kind of morning I'll work twice through the gearbox
just to drive one block, just pleased
to know a hand is at the end of my arm.

Or maybe there's rain and I can see it slant with the air,
maybe some French Canadian singer on the radio
is helping me hear English for the first time,
and the percussion is being supplied by the roof —
maybe the wipers can't work fast enough.

Anything, anything to feel connected
(and you haven't heard anything until you've heard
a French-speaking disc jockey say something in Chinese),
though it doesn't last long, can't, apparently
and I end up shifting down

like when you're smiling and stop
and your face melts down a little, following
the momentum, hits a curb as you park
and you feel your face then,
all it's made of.

What is a face? What muscles relaxing
over what bones as I enter the establishment,
or better, *whose* face is so distorted,
as in the heat of a desert, in the mirror, above
and behind the coffee maker I'm heading for?

In *The Last Emperor*, the last emperor of China
is a three-year-old the court can't look at directly
and growing up he plays a game with the palace eunuchs.
They hold yards of silk cloth between themselves and him
and he touches their faces through it, trying to guess

who is what but it takes him years and years to learn
to get to know his own face — feel the canvas as it moves,
like backdrop scenery by a stage door's opening and closing,
and know that it's the way his life has moved,
that life has to shift like a face,
that there's no system to the desert,
and he's been like sand sliding down a hill of sand.

Oh lovers, let's get up and go to 7–11:
like the city, we live mere inches
above an empire of bones,
the true body,
where the walls are even thicker than motel room curtains,
and the light won't keep traveling from the sleeping face.

If the Prunes Don't Get You,
Then the Apricots Must

Everything is somewhat other, today. The maple tree
with its dozen mossy armpits, for instance,
and the little woodpecker that reminds me of my father
singing "Good Morning Mr. Zip Zip Zip." Even the lawn,
which looks silly in its hair net —
there are maybe ten cowlicks I missed mowing it —
and the two cars in front of the garage like slippers
next to a bedside table. The sky, in fact, has already
smeared some sort of cream all over its face, branches
brush its teeth, and the light has a soapy glint to it.
But why is nature going to bed at ten in the morning?
Why do even the shrubs, which always look like they just got up,
seem called to bed right back down?

When I was a kid, my mother would break imaginary eggs
over my hair, letting her fingers run down my scalp
after my cousins tossed me, literally, from one Dutch rub
to another. It was their fault
when I decided to let my hair grow out
and then had to sleep with hosiery on my head.
Everybody I knew had two feet and used them: my mother's arms
had not turned thin and bony like collapsed umbrellas,
the fir joists in her body had not warped and sprung,
my father had not plummeted into the tall grass I can't get to
because of the roots, like a pine cone.

I think maybe it's because I'm such a tree today
and would like to lie down, but can't.
I have a duty to what is perched
and depending on me. Did I ever show you my photo of then?
My bangs arched out like the eave of a roof,
my nose never got wet till I was sixteen. Will you feel this

lump and tell me what it is? I had several little ones
and now there's one big one. Sweetheart,
I'm not going anywhere today —
something's been sleeping beneath my bed, and my,
what awfully big teeth it has.

Running My Fingers Through
My Beard on Bolton Road

I've been thinking about the women who've kissed me,
I've been thinking a lot about them, and I've decided
that my mouth is nothing to be ashamed of. Like when
I mow the lawn and uncover the old elm stump we put
back in the ground. We said it was to help us split
the rest of the elm, but knew it was a sort of homage.

What goes around comes around, is one way of saying it.
Another is to answer, "Yes, you are pretty and I want you,"
after seven years, even though I say it
into another woman's ear. My beard has heard

all this before. The messiness of that hunger,
the memory of it. Sometimes it seems white
in the light I wake up to, but I am a young man,
something I tell my old dog when he's acted badly,
a horrible thing to say, "I will outlive you." Maybe, maybe not,
but probably

destined to. The way the way the papergirl hugged herself all
winter could not hold back her breasts. I watched her trudging
through those months in an adolescent stupor and I loved her,
wanted to bring her galoshes and tell her that one day
she would wake up and reconcile herself with this neighborhood,
and walk about freely in her memory of it with nothing to deliver
but her sweet, sweet self, and that then she'd maybe smile a little,
remember how I always ran the stop sign just as she had three more
houses to go and . . .

But then spring sprang and I found my car veering toward her,
as it does toward unusual, beautiful other cars, and for a second I
didn't love her anymore, just *wanted* somehow, and was ashamed. Or

did I? Was I? I don't know. There are so many men out here, waiting
to be saved from the awful shapelessness of the air around them. I
for one, cannot tell you how much I need breasts, and mouths,
and questions like the ones you asked me. I can't explain
the ambiguous way my mother and my father's mistress coexisted
behind the buttons of your shirts. Or how I can close my eyes
and imagine the hay-yellow light of evening on my grandmother's
self-conscious face. How, though that newly raised barn is
gone, though the fiddle music which was just beginning
is gone, though every person who was there is gone, still,
a soft-faced boy raises one foot and begins to step toward her.

Child or woman. Memory or need. Today, again, I can see you
in her eyes, today her eyes again pursue the ground, look
for some sign, some path to follow away from her route.
Her sweatshirt is zipped to the throat and I am realizing that
we are both then, somehow ashamed of what has suddenly happened
between us. And I'm slowing down a little, as if to let
the spring sun catch up to these hands on the steering wheel,
these hands that will not ever stop needing breasts to
make them hands, as if to uncover my mouth
and yell across the lawns to her.

It's wrong to not know how beautiful you are.
I shouldn't make too much of this, but all month
I've passed a boy in Vernon. He has track shoes slung
over his shoulder and cigarette smoke trailing out of his mouth,
like he'll never make up his mind.
It should come as no surprise, but he *is* walking south.
And there is something he has to ask you.

Why Is That Pencil
Always Behind Your Ear

I lay soaking into the bench, getting whiter and whiter,
getting it wrong. I laid on the beach with a hotel
for a tombstone, trying to think of our country
as one big old house with the sea for a backyard.

Some other kids were shoveling holes everywhere
and their dog, which had been frantically planting his flag
on the shore, and which had finally given up all hope
of leaving some trace of himself, laid down too,
and waited for them to finish. So I knew

then why some are said to howl at the moon.
It *is* a sort of madness. It's being the only dog
on a long stretch of beach — with shards of a foreign life
jammed up into the pads of your feet. No wonder

he took such interest, later, when the gulls lowered
like a mobile and he saw the single black crow
walking speechless among them. He must have thought,
Oh comrade, the stories we could tell each other.

Maybe it was a fugitive from justice. Maybe it was rich
and bored. Or maybe it was just a dreamer grown tired
of the dead in the road. I couldn't tell you. But
you've been lost, haven't you? And you too may have a
piece of No. 3 lead in your thigh that has been there

practically forever. Sometimes at work I'll drop my tools,
and in the instant it takes to pick them up, I'll feel the
ghost of a pencil behind my ear. A small, insistent pressure,
perhaps a little like the bunching of a dog's ribs

just before it barks. Or the wind catching beneath
a folded black wing. It recedes, but doesn't go away.
And it leaves the T-shirts and the lime shorts,
the flip-flops and the togs and the toys, the blue jeans

with black thighs where we've rubbed our hands. As if
someone else's life had just receded, leaving you your own.
Which is why, though the point snaps again and again,
I have to keep doing this.

Now the light inches down that hotel's face like tidewater.
Shortly, the crabs can come out again and be safe on their many legs,
the oysters can surface to try once more to spit out the pearls
they hate so much. Oh comrade, the stories we'll tell each other.

River

The harbor is a place I think of you.
It's good to stand staring at the sea
without having to turn my back on anything.
To love you, to love being here in my beige shirt;
all this is is loving myself for a little while.

The wind coming toward me off the water,
the wind in my shirttail like a flag, my
collar tips like small wings at my throat.
Some people get thirsty when they look at the sea —
me, I always feel like I have one breath
to tell you my whole life with.

So many lights on the water.
When I come here at night
it's like coming to a mirror to dress:
at the right distance I can see me wholly.
Everything comes back. The waves,

they bring it all back
and lay it at your feet so you can see it —
a little weathered maybe, a little more polished
or broken than you remembered, but all of it.

Always, across the bay, so many different sets of warning lights.
One for the bridge, another for the water tower, and so on.
I used to warm my hands on them in the early morning
when I painted such things — have a smoke, get myself together
as the fog burned off. Depending on the hangover, I was either

very big or very small up there. Matters of perspective maybe,
but of life and death too, the way these sparks across the harbor
seem reflections of those beacons
but aren't — just pleasure boats, or shrimpers
with some red in their running lights.

I'm out here for the same reason they are;
I just want to be nearby what I love most.
It got windy today so I drank,
(they fill water towers to the brim during hurricanes,
they're engineered like that,

and sometimes I think I am too —
though I'm a little short, admittedly,
and not half as useful in an emergency),
and now my legs are sad as concrete footings;
I'm here to stay.

I just want to be loved back by what I love most:
the little feelings I'll reel in — the big ones I won't;
tin cans (aluminum only lasts about six weeks at sea);
a piece of tire from a pier; little snatches of newspaper
I can't read anymore: memories of coming to at back tables

and finding my wallet still in my pocket; or of waking
atop sand hoppers that rose
through cloverleaf overpass interchanges —
seeing the St. Louis rush hour eye to eye . . .
Here. There. Blame it on the Mississippi in each of us.

At lunch, up there, lying leaning aginst the tank or the bridge
with my feet hung over the rail, I made believe it was a ship
and the stiff wind was taking me down the river.
It could have been any city when I looked out and down then,
still chewing on a sandwich, thinking, if I could only be
in the same room with you, feel you looking at me
the way I felt the neighbors' binoculars.

But I'm just standing here on a pier, what do I know.
And that's the outside, anyway — inside a water tower
is a different story, it's like a cave you enter out of fear
and then get stuck in. Once, at the bottom of a riser,
I stripped off all my clothes,

I stood there in my underwear, terrified that I'd misjudged
my whole life and when I came out of that hole
I felt like I was new.
That passes also. There are passages through the self
too small to get through. Pretty soon there's no metaphor in it,
no analogy, nothing but work and money to drink with,
nothing to drink from anymore.

But I was talking about the ocean, wasn't I.

Long-lighted Evenings in the Garden

I go out mornings and put my hand on the hood
but it's never warm anymore. Just an old homebody
with my eyes closed nights. Still, I saw another
blue truck this afternoon and for a light-change
thought it was me leaning into that turn.
I considered rolling down my window to yell at myself,
but of course, I can hear me quite well
without making a spectacle of it.

What I remember is how we pulled into the driveway at the same time
and I was surprised. You looked different alone, in the car, outside
the apartment — like a woman just stopping for directions.
It's kind of nice to feel so separate and yet so attached.

From here, the stars are a handful of white gravel
on that asphalt in Illinois, a shock seeding
of determined white rain on the windshield of a planet
that's late for its own wedding. How we do move through space!
Nope. Space moves around us. We're like flickering orange cones
and space is continually taking a driver's test.
That's why there's always a breeze here on these cool, long-lighted
evenings in the garden.

About the pickup: I almost followed it, almost drove west instead
of home. Then I knew I didn't want to know.

Rubbing Dirt from My Dog's Nose, I Realize

I'm not crazed with loving, I don't see you
whenever I close my eyes, anymore.
When I think of us, it's like looking at my shoes
through a glass coffee table —
if I can reach the laces at all,
I tie them in another world
and my first thought is whose hands are those?

I don't see my own face, even
when my nose is scarcely an inch
above the glass,
and I can lean back then,
blunt my cigarette in the ashtray,
and remain completely alone.

I remember the snow though, can you?
In another hour or so, we knew, it
would be pushed to the sides of the road,
and piled there to freeze and melt and freeze
so that it would hurt to have to walk through that snow again,
to remember it now.

Knowing that, all I wanted was for you to say
you saw the same things I did:
how the sparse weeds bristled at the base of the hill,
and the snow seemed to fall in front
of the town below us,

like in one of those low-budget films
where each actor knows just how badly things are going
but keeps doing his or her job, listening
to the prerecorded barking

of dogs that have been bones for years,
and the muffled scrape of snow scoops long since
curled up into rust.

It was so still, and yet you had to tell me
when I dropped my keys.
Pine trees leaned into each other and
their branches touched the ground.
A squirrel jabbed its head into the snow.
By afternoon, there would be so much
that people getting off work would have to guess
which car they held the key to.
In the same way that when I close my eyes now
I can almost miss even the idea of you.

I just realized I've never actually seen my dog bury anything
at all, but squirrels do, and certain species of trees feel gratitude
when they forget just where.

It's the same sort of difference,
and forty years from now
that's probably all there'll be to it:
I'll look at snow and fill with something that's just like snow,
one flake will land between my hair and my collar,
and I'll have to lean against who's near me.
It's how I'll stand not even having you to bear.

Back Pressure

One year and five months to the day
and this waiting room
where I'm still picking scabs of paint from my watch.
The first color handed me was yellow, and when
I quit, I made sure I ended with yellow,
and put my foot down on the lid
and stood on it —
it took all the weight I had to quit that job.
I look at the time again — it's twenty past yellow.

Last week Rita said my breath smelled like lacquer,
and she hadn't thought she'd ever have to say that
again. Today the doctor will remind me
of all the permanent damage done to my lungs
and ask me how in God's name I can keep on smoking.

Once a friend asked, did I have three buttons sewn
to the sleeves of my suit? Did I know what
they were for? Napoleon ordered their issue
to keep his men from wiping their noses on his uniforms.
He said, "Do you realize how slowly humans change."

Well, I can walk into any room and still notice
how it was painted, and with what. The mistakes,
the sly shortcuts, still make me feel what's missing.
There is great pleasure to be had
from the small thing well done. Teaching
seems always to be so big,
and I do good so rarely . . .
but what soft hands I have with which to massage my temples.
Most of the calluses gone. As are all
my friends from that time.

Levered off with a scraper, the lid
peels back slowly, as if on hinges,
and there you are, 8:04 in the A.M.,
staring through a porthole
at the rest of your well-paying life —
a career of color-coding pipes,
while never being quite sure
of just what they convey.

They begin and end at machines and reservoirs;
they disappear into the ceilings, hug the walls;
they flare, expand, and diminish;
they converge and disperse, while you have your
one room, or your one floor to trace utterly,
complete, and pronounce designated
in accordance with the schema decreed.

Is it properly accomplished? Is it up to spec?
Will the painters of some future moment
curse you or willingly follow the original strokes
of a brush they've been handed as if it were torch?

Blues, browns, greens, greys —
you would not believe how beautiful black is
in the can: lustrous, sexy;
red can cause the most washed-out soul
to lean with more force than necessary
against one rung of the ladder,
but black can make people forget about lunch.

I didn't clean the brush, I just soaked it in thinner;
I picked up my bag without counting my tools,
rolled my shirts up in my pants
and walked away, offering my badge
to the guard shack's counter
like a slap in the face.

But, one year and five months, to the day,
I find I'm not gone, just still leaving. Someone
skipped the baseboard under the radiator by the window —
twice. Someone missed five inches of the edge of the door.

Simile at the Side of the Road

In photographs of our galaxy
it looks like someone's just finished
stirring us with a long wooden spoon
like someone has the lid in one hand
head bowed into the steam
trying to figure out what it needs

like when your car overheats
and you open the hood
awestruck
with self-conscious ignorance
on a forming universe
to fiddle with important-looking things

while to schmucks passing at 70
which of course is illegal for good reason
(since one envies them now)
it looks like Rod Serling just got a good grip on your hair
and is pulling the upper half of your body into the Twilight Zone

though you're still there
of course
a fact of which
the small children pushing each other around
in the backseat are incessantly reminding you
and though the neuroses hurtling through the back of your head
have had to dim their lights
lost as you are
in a helplessly complex assemblage of archetypal shapes and shadings
with grease on your hands

(knowing well it will soon be on your face
inspiring dreams of ninjadom and pillage
at Babe's Pre-Owned Cars)

but leaving the war goop and camouflage wallet aside
(never point a loaded flour sifter
unless you plan on using it)

and getting back to that nice homey
mm-mm good soup metaphor
you know that you will really be in it
if you're late for work again today
so you grate your teeth
try once more to rub the Parmesan from your eyes
and think

the whole point being
that the kid scribbling crayon on your interior
can't write notes for *you*
and it's this
not looking at the Milky Way slowly cooling and clearing
against the black backdrop of hood insulation
that makes you feel so small

Tell Us Everything You Know

In that life, mornings were questions I refused
to answer. The clock threw water in my face. My job
chain-smoked behind intense light. Low voices, stiff shoes,
lined up behind the one-way glass
at the bottom of the glass
and still, I kept my mouth shut.
Not one thin dream between me and the scuffed linoleum
of sleep, not one note smuggled in from anywhere.
Are you a human being, they asked? Where were you
the night the world disappeared . . . Will anyone remember
seeing you? Can you supply us with a list,
or at least a lover who will lie for you?

Often as not, I'd wake up too fast, swearing
I'd been knifed. Anyway, I'd hold myself like that,
like some unforgettable sunset
leaking through the fingers of my hands.
We're not going anywhere, they said.
We've got nothing but time, they said.

If I were an American Indian my name would be Registers Slowly,
but I uncrossed my arms one morning and admitted
that people can't bury themselves.
And when I saw my hands around the tumbler I drank from,
they could have been anybody's hands. And when I saw
each tick and tock in the molding, the shining black
where someone else's shoes had rubbed against the door leading out,
when I smelled the loneliness of the last few drops of tonic
in the bottle in the corner,

I held myself like *that*. And wept like that.
And confessed how I'd so often been ready to talk,
that it was never necessary to defend myself,
that the weight of the world can't be carried by six people,
but has to be
and is.

How Can I Be Out of Danger
If I'm Not Dead

Lately I'm happy when I get up. Lately I go straight
to the window and part the flimsy metal blinds
like I'm expecting a birth of some sort.
Or I plant my feet, wiggle my butt, and say "Hike,"
peering in, astonished, as if that's where I kept my money
and there's more there than I figured. But
yesterday
the dawn was so stark that the sky was still dark enough
to make the triple-paned thermo-sealed glass reflect everything.
I saw an infantile head and it looked like me!
It scared me so bad that I stopped thinking about vaginas!
So I got down on my knees where I could no longer see myself
and said, "Just tell me what it's like where you are."

That's how it goes, hating your best friend. Knowing
he'll be jealous and want to kill you when you fall in love
with somebody else. Knowing you can stay forever on one knee
drawing intricate plays in the dirt with your finger
and he'll still read you every time and knock you down
and take your wallet and leave you fifty cents for a Twinkie.
Knowing you'll never be safe!
But lately we keep getting up. And I seem pretty happy about it.

The Shear Pin of You

When I put my face into this water until my ears fill with it,
the night world establishes its glassy distance.
Everything feels far off and sounds lost and unreachable,
everything looks so close that I can at last enclose it. Here
the blazing white propellor of my twenties settles
between stones thick with sea moss and the anchors wear thin
on their brave ropes and I can scuttle a little,
move any direction immediately. You know, I'm still amazed
when I put my hand into this sea and feel the chain on its plug.
That I can do this is miraculous and dreamy, like when

the lobster pot dreams
of being pulled up
by the sure hands of a light it
can barely remember — back to where
it catches a glimpse of a windbreak,
or a branch of wooden pier,
so that its breath comes into it
like something sharp and mysterious, important enough
so that even the lobster, not quite inside, still refuses
to let go and breaks water for the first time —
breaks through to its future, which is

being in a stomach, both fulfilled
and back where it started, while static
gradually recedes into music and the maples beside
Route 6 turn and lower and raise their solemn heads
as the U-Haul full of furniture barrels north
by northwestward like a flight of geese and I follow

that continual series of wakes into waking,
the water of which now runs down my face
toward the channel of my breastbone where, if you listen,
there is still the far-submerged roar of a life churning
and a keel rising and falling, and love somehow,
though small in that cold expanse, driving
its one root even deeper.

Spoons

You are a mirror for my life now;
when I look at you
I see my wife and me in the bed across the room,

my clothes on her clothes on clothes hooks,
the TV still warm
when I reach over and place the empty bowl on top.

One spoon in the whole house,
just like I wanted,
one real thing to chew on till I die, like my dog

who has never let loose of the squeaky gift
you gave it,
will bury anything but that.

It's enough sometimes; I never dreamed
that the ideal
could be so functional. Now, it moves me

to see my wife roll over and into sleep,
tired from a long day
of surviving her life. She likes to sleep with

one hand partially raised, which she explains
her first husband's violence
probably branded in her genes. It's enough,

in fact more than that, though our language
is averse to words like "enough" and "ordinary."
I don't want you

because I have you and have stopped needing
to be with you.
How vulnerable you are, now that I won't die for you;

suddenly, I want to protect you and make love to my wife.

New Construction

Stars like bits of glass in the sole of a shoe,
one cloud crossing the broken window, it's like this
that friends' thoughts pass one to another —

as if there's something old in us that can barely be touched.
When I held my goddaughter for the first time,
peeled the blanket from her forehead, kissed her blank face,

it was with the feeling I get standing on a ladder
with just my head in the attic, or looking down
the stairwells of old buildings. Something swayed in me,

something I've been built around. And then she stretched —
the way when I was alone, my dog put his feet against the wall,
pushed the length of his spine against my own —

and there was something behind her voice, a little growl,
when her mother held out her arms and asked for her,
like a sleepy lover asking what time it was.

➤

I straightened, did something small. I reversed the pencil
behind my ear, returned some chewed gum to its wrapper.
There were trains beneath me, winds above me, arroyos
of clarity and shadow between the buildings beside me.

I wanted to say something that would fireproof her life
the way I once sprayed new girders and decks for a living.
I wanted to tell her that when it's put on too thick
it breaks off like shale, that when you work up

above the twenties you feel the sway more, have to pry
the bare plywood back one corner at a time, lean back
into a bundle of sheetrock, and look out over your coffee
to keep from thinking about the ground.

➤

But by that time we'd regressed to "goo" and "ga"
and taken shelter in a store whose window was a blur
of all the jackets and umbrellas we didn't own and
wherein no one could seem to get over how good it smelled
since there were fifty kinds of coffee on the shelves of the place.

I think that was the first time she'd felt rain on her face
and couldn't quite decide whether she liked it or not.
Her eyes were squinched shut and when I kissed her good-bye,
she opened them, as if to remind me
that the first thing in the morning *is* the morning;
that we die every day and wake alive, not so much reborn
as torn away from dying by someone's lips on our own.

And that even as buildings bow to the strain,
down each hall, each door bears its polished number.

Donald

When chimpanzees are threatened, they band together at first
and touch their hands to each others' mouths
as if to say, "Yes, I'm here."

Something like the way a man might find himself
hurrying down the hall, running
a callused thumb over his kid's lips, saying,
"I know you're afraid," again, again, and again,
even after the child has leaned back into the limbs of sleep.

The chimps will then venture out, away from the group —
on land in the savannah,
across the tree, in the trees —
and throw what they can at their enemy in an underhand motion,
or break off sticks and approach it.

Today at work, in the washroom mirror,
while I was trying to get the water in my cupped hands to my face
without spilling any,
I saw little smears of paint everywhere
and realized how often I'd touched my own face during the day:
a decision in front of the candy machine; rubbing my eyes,
the bridge of my nose. Though I didn't know,

it rained all morning and into afternoon while I painted
the superstructure of the ceiling of that factory, by which
means now, strapped in and idling next to the 7-11,
my hand inside a small paper bag,
listening to the new silence of a new exhaust system,
the almost-evening summer light seems clean here on the parking lot.

From outside, through the glass of the windshield
and then the glass of the storefront,
half-clearly and half-convoluted
by the reflection of both bars across the street,
I can see a kid in a tuxedo, his hands two bulges
in the pockets of his pants, smiling at the counterman.

If I didn't know him, he could be just any young guy
holding his head in such a way it's obvious
his shirt neck's too tight;
but I do, and I know
the graft marks on the side of his face that isn't towards me
and I know the thick, kind speech that betrays brain damage.

His date is in there too, fussing now and again
with his chopped hair — a pretty woman, tall, fluid, sure
when she parked the car and got out a minute ago. And I've found
what I was feeling in the bag for, and I'm in reverse now,
backing up from the window, trying to enjoy one of those smiles
one smiles remembering something,

when they appear wholly, carrying nothing,
while the counterman neglects a customer to watch them do so,
and as the boy walks along the sidewalk, across the entryway
he's swept and shoveled out a thousand times,
he turns the leathery, gasoline-seared left side of his face,
and turning her attention once more to the hair above its ear,
she touches him briefly there.

I'm turning the wheel with the flat palm of one hand,
scratching (which is a sign of indecision in chimps)
my chest with the cold root beer in my other,
and hesitating at the exit, thinking I could so easily
get sad now, because I know it's his sister,
but when I look in the rearview mirror, look back, I can see
that his friend who works nights has come out to wave,

and think instead of how always the chimps return to touch
and be touched again, that if you were here, you'd know
what I was about to say, and as if you were here, I feel, bringing
the cool rim of that can to my lips, your fingers and pull away.

The Will

I am about to — or, I am going to — die:
either expression is correct.

> —Dominique Bouhours
> (French grammarian, d. 1702)

Tilting my head, watching car lights wind
down the mountain, I realize
how easily the mountain moves.
It's in flames on the glass of our window,
like our faces in those flames,
while the one cloud, backlit, and pausing
briefly along the top of the mountain,
rains out there beyond us,
yet inside us too.

What we have is here to be seen through.
Cinnamon tea welling in our spoons,
steam rising
off the dog still trembling near the hearth —
we've made plans.

I sought for a town among mountains, once;
a little Greek town where the wind
would put its soft mouth to the houses
in the one chord I could sleep to.
When the windows chattered restless in casings there,
it would feel good to shiver in the dark with them.
And upon closing my eyes I would see through the earth
and fall to a space where time ruled so gently
that the stars could cease their blinking. A car
turning the corner could lay its white hand on my forehead,
but I'd know it was God.

" 'Light! More light!' " you ask,
"Whose last words were those?"
Then, " 'Put out that bloody cigarette . . .' "
which were H. H. Munro's. How easily
that German bullet translated his individuated voice,
even as he attempted to stay entrenched in the dark.

Today, when the dog dropped your stick
at my feet, and shook the lake from himself
I was shocked by the cold he'd just as soon return to.
But when I looked at the water it was a Greek woman

standing and smoothing her dress, and I knew
that wherever we're going it won't be cold at all,
it won't be permanent. The wavering, the flickering,
the motion is what matters.

Notes

p. 3   "The Word" is for Stephen Berg and partially owes its shape to his "On This Side of the River."

p. 20   "I Want to Know What Love Is" takes its title from a song by Foreigner. Line nine is adapted from Yeats's "When You Are Old."

p. 24   The line "the tearing and merging of clouds" is the title of a poem by Russell Edson.

p. 32   "Keepers" is for Jack and Jacob Myers.

p. 35   "Divorce" is for Ben Mitchell.

p. 45   The quotation bridging the first and second stanzas on this page is paraphrased from Marcel Proust's *Remembrance of Things Past*.

p. 60   "Back Pressure" is for Gordon Weaver.

p. 67   "How Can I Be Out of Danger if I'm Not Dead" takes its title from a line of dialogue in the movie *Rachel, Rachel*.

ABOUT THE AUTHOR

Mark Cox was born in 1956 and raised in Belleville, Illinois. He received his B.A. from DePauw University and his M.F.A. from Vermont College. He worked as an industrial painter for many years and now teaches writing and literature at Goddard College and in the Master of Fine Arts in Writing program of Vermont College. The recipient of a Whiting Award and a fellowship from the Vermont Council on the Arts, his poems have appeared in such magazines as *The American Poetry Review, The North American Review, Poetry,* and *Poetry Northwest.*

SMOULDER

has been set in a film version of Electra by PennSet, Inc. of Blooms-
burg, Pennsylvania. Designed by William Addison Dwiggins for the
Mergenthaler Linotype Company and first made available in 1935,
Electra is impossible to classify as either "modern" or "old-style."
Not based on any historical model or reflecting any particular period
or style, it is notable for its clean and elegant lines, its lack of contrast
between the thick and thin elements that characterizes most
modern faces, and its freedom from all idiosyncrasies
that catch the eye and interfere with reading.

Printed and bound by Maple-Vail Book
Manufacturing Group, Binghamton, New York.
Designed by Lisa Clark